# The Importance of Honesty

Stories that show the value of telling the truth, even when it's difficult, and the consequences of lying.

Written by Jeremy Kilth

Copyright (c) 2024

# Foreword

Welcome to the first book in a series designed to guide young minds through the vast and vibrant landscape of moral values. "The Importance of Honesty," our inaugural volume, serves as the cornerstone of this exciting journey into understanding and practicing key moral principles.

In this collection, we dive into the world of honesty - a virtue fundamental to the fabric of trust and integrity. Through five captivating stories, children will explore various scenarios where truth plays the pivotal role. They will meet characters who face the temptation to deceive, and witness the repercussions of their choices, learning along the way that honesty is not just the best policy, but the foundation of meaningful and lasting relationships.

But our journey does not end here. "The Importance of Honesty" is the first stepping stone in a broader path we will walk together, exploring nine more moral themes. Each subsequent book will unravel stories about kindness, sharing, perseverance, empathy, teamwork, patience, caution, generosity, and forgiveness. These themes have been carefully chosen to nurture empathy, understanding, and ethical reasoning in our young readers, helping them grow into thoughtful, compassionate, and responsible individuals.

As these tales of moral values unfold, my goal is to spark conversations between children and their guardians, educators, and peers. I hope to encourage discussions that go beyond the pages, fostering an environment where these moral lessons are not only learned but lived.

So, let us embark on this journey together, starting with the powerful truth of honesty. May these stories resonate with our young readers, illuminating their paths with the wisdom to make choices that will shape a brighter, more compassionate world.

With warm regards,

Jeremy Kilth, Author and Creator of the Moral Values Series

# TABLE OF CONTENTS

Foreword ........................................................................................................ 3

**The Boy and the Shiny Whistle** ................................................................ 6
    The Discovery in the Park .................................................................... 6
    Whispers of Worry ................................................................................ 6
    The Sound of Conscience .................................................................... 7
    Echoes of Courage ................................................................................ 8
    A New Tune ............................................................................................ 9
    Reflection .............................................................................................. 11

**The Test Day Mix-Up** ............................................................................... 12
    Ava's Discovery .................................................................................... 12
    The Night of Choices .......................................................................... 13
    The Truth Unfolds ............................................................................... 14
    Reflection .............................................................................................. 16

**The Farmer's Missing Apples** ................................................................ 18
    The Orchard Adventure ..................................................................... 18
    The Missing Apples ............................................................................. 19
    The Weight of Truth ........................................................................... 20
    Reflection .............................................................................................. 22

**The Artist's Signature** ............................................................................ 23
    A Canvas of Possibilities .................................................................... 23
    The Unclaimed Masterpiece ............................................................. 24
    Colors of Confrontation ..................................................................... 25
    The Palette of Truth ........................................................................... 27
    Reflection .............................................................................................. 29

**The Whispered Rumor** ...................................................................... 31
    **The Monster's Birth** ................................................................ 31
    **The Whispers Grow** ............................................................... 32
    **The Courage to Confess** ........................................................ 33
    **Reflection** ................................................................................ 35

# The Boy and the Shiny Whistle

## The Discovery in the Park

In the hazy glow of late summer, when shadows stretched long and the air hummed with the laughter of children playing, Jamie skipped along the path that wound through the neighborhood park. The sun winked through the leaves, dappling the ground with patches of light and warmth, teasing the day to linger just a little longer.

The park was Jamie's kingdom, a place of endless wonder, where every tree whispered secrets and every breeze carried tales of adventure. He knew each hidden nook and familiar cranny, but today, something unusual caught his eye.

Nestled between two roots of the old oak tree, something shiny beckoned him. Jamie, with the boundless curiosity of an 8-year-old, dashed over and plucked the object from the grass. It was a whistle, unlike any he had ever seen—silvery and cool to the touch, with a little star etched onto its side. He grinned, the corners of his mouth stretching wide as the park itself.

With a quick glance around, as if the trees themselves might tell on him, Jamie slipped the whistle into his pocket. The thrill of the find sent a shiver of excitement dancing down his spine. He could hardly wait to show his friends the treasure he'd discovered.

As he made his way home, Jamie took the whistle out and admired it in the fading light. The whistle seemed to sing to him, a siren's call that promised grand tales and playful days. And Jamie, with a heart as open as the sky above, was all too happy to answer its call.

## Whispers of Worry

The new day dawned, painting the sky in streaks of pink and gold. Jamie woke with the sun, his mind still dancing with the image of the shiny whistle. Today, he decided, would be the day he shared his find with the neighborhood.

After breakfast, he met his friends at the park, their faces alight with the boundless energy that only a fresh day could bring. "Look what I found!"

Jamie exclaimed, his voice trembling with barely contained excitement. He produced the whistle from his pocket with a magician's flair.

The whistle's luster seemed to cast a spell over the group, their eyes wide with awe. They passed it around, each one blowing into it, creating a symphony of sharp notes that sailed through the air. Jamie, in the center of the circle, basked in the warmth of his friends' admiration. He was the hero of the hour, the boy with the whistle that sang of mystery and magic.

But the winds of fortune are ever fickle. As the day rolled on, hushed tones began to drift among the children. Mr. Harrison, the kindly old man who was a fixture of the neighborhood with his daily walks, was looking for something. He walked slower than usual, his usual bright smile dimmed by a shadow of concern.

"He's lost his whistle," one of the kids whispered, a furrow of worry creasing their brow. "He says it keeps him safe."

The words, simple and soft, struck Jamie like a clap of thunder. His heart, which had fluttered with joy, now felt heavy, the whistle in his pocket burning like a coal. He watched from afar as Mr. Harrison searched, his usual cheerful whistle replaced by a silence that seemed to echo too loudly.

Jamie's friends looked to him, their eyes reflecting the sun's last rays, but all he could see was the crestfallen slump of Mr. Harrison's shoulders. The whistle, once a beacon of excitement, now felt like an anchor, pulling him down into a sea of guilt.

As the sun dipped below the horizon, Jamie's inner turmoil cast a longer shadow than the oak tree that had hidden the whistle. The joy of discovery had been replaced by the whisper of worry, and the night couldn't come fast enough to cloak his troubled thoughts.

## The Sound of Conscience

Under the silver watch of the moon, the neighborhood slept peacefully, a blanket of tranquility laid upon every lawn and street. But in Jamie's room, the shadows seemed to move with the weight of his thoughts, and the silence was heavy with unspoken words.

The whistle lay on his nightstand, the star engraving catching the moonlight and throwing specks of light across the darkened room. It was as if the whistle was calling out, not with sound, but with the burden of truth that now rested on Jamie's young shoulders.

At breakfast, Jamie's parents noticed the change in him. Where there was usually a bright-eyed boy full of chatter, there now sat a silent shadow of their son. "Is everything alright, Jamie?" his mother asked, her voice a soft melody of concern.

"Just tired," Jamie murmured, pushing his cereal around the bowl, each spoonful as heavy as the words lodged in his throat. His parents exchanged a look over the top of his head, a silent conversation of worry, but they didn't press further.

That day, the park's vibrant life seemed distant to Jamie. The laughter of his friends sounded muffled, as if he were hearing it from underwater. His secret was a stone in his pocket, growing heavier with each passing hour.

When Mr. Harrison passed by on his walk, slower and more somber than before, the usual friendly greeting was absent. Instead, a quiet nod was all he offered before continuing on his way. Jamie watched him go, the familiar sound of the shiny whistle painfully absent.

As twilight approached, Jamie sat alone on the swing, the cold metal of the whistle now a stark reminder of Mr. Harrison's lonely figure. The stars began to peek through the dusky sky, but their sparkle brought no comfort. It was the star on the whistle that held Jamie's gaze, a stark reminder of the stark truth he had yet to face.

The whistle seemed to grow louder in the silence, its call a clear note amidst the cacophony of his inner turmoil. And in the quiet of the coming night, with the stars as his witnesses, Jamie knew what he must do. It was time for the truth to be as free as the sound that once echoed joyfully through the park.

## Echoes of Courage

As dawn crept across the sky, painting it with the promise of a new beginning, Jamie lay awake. The first chirps of waking birds filtered through his window, a reminder that the world was moving forward, as he must too.

With the decision made in the solitude of night now pressing upon him, Jamie rose. He dressed silently, the whistle's weight in his pocket a constant reminder of the day's impending confession.

He found Mr. Harrison on his morning walk, the path familiar under his feet but different somehow, as if each step was a note in a song of redemption. Mr. Harrison's face, lined with the gentle marks of time, was turned to the morning sun, perhaps seeking the warmth of a day not shadowed by loss.

"Mr. Harrison," Jamie's voice broke the morning's silence, softer than he intended but carried by the crisp air.

The old man turned, his surprise at seeing Jamie there so early evident in the lift of his eyebrows. "Good morning, Jamie. What brings you out with the larks?"

Jamie's hand found the whistle in his pocket, the cool metal a stark contrast to his warm, nervous fingers. He drew a deep breath, the same breath that had given life to the whistle's sound now steadying his voice.

"I have something that belongs to you," Jamie began, his words tumbling out like the first drops of a needed rain. He held out the whistle, its surface catching the morning light, a beacon of his truth.

Mr. Harrison's eyes widened, a mix of emotions crossing his face. He took the whistle gently, his touch reverent. For a moment, the park held its breath, the trees standing witness to the boy's act of bravery.

Jamie waited, the echoes of courage still vibrating in the air. Mr. Harrison looked at him, the silence stretching between them not with judgment, but with understanding. And in the soft light of morning, with the courage of honesty lighting his way, Jamie felt the weight lifting, replaced by an unfamiliar lightness—the buoyancy of integrity.

"I'm sorry," Jamie added, the words unnecessary but important, another step on the path he chose to walk—a path of honor that was only just beginning.

## A New Tune

Mr. Harrison's face softened into a gentle, understanding smile, the lines around his eyes crinkling like the pages of a well-loved storybook. He placed a hand on Jamie's shoulder, grounding him in the gravity of the moment.

"Jamie, you've done a brave thing today," Mr. Harrison said, his voice a quiet melody of kindness. "It takes courage to admit when we've made a mistake. You've shown great honesty."

The whistle, now back in the hands of its owner, seemed to gleam a little brighter, as if polished by the act of righteousness. Mr. Harrison lifted the whistle to his lips and blew a short, sweet note that danced through the air and twirled around Jamie, lifting the last remnants of his worry like leaves in a playful wind.

Jamie's heart swelled with a symphony of relief and pride. The fear of reprimand had dissipated, replaced by the harmonious chords of Mr. Harrison's forgiveness and wisdom.

"And now," Mr. Harrison continued, a twinkle in his eye, "this whistle has an even greater story to tell—one of lost and found, and of a young boy who did the right thing."

Together, they walked back through the park, the same path Jamie had trodden countless times, now new and enlightened by the truth. Mr. Harrison shared tales of his own youthful adventures, of mistakes made and lessons learned, a shared rhythm between the past and present.

As they approached the heart of the park where their paths would part, Mr. Harrison stopped and turned to Jamie. "You've given me more than just a whistle today. You've given me hope. Hope in the goodness that the next generation holds."

With the rising sun casting a golden light on the new day, Jamie felt as if he had grown, not in size, but in spirit. He understood now that honesty was more than a word; it was a melody to live by, a tune that would guide him through the complexities of life with a clear and steadfast beat.

And as he waved goodbye to Mr. Harrison, Jamie knew that this was not an ending but a beginning—the first note of his own story of integrity, a tale that he would add to with each choice he made. It was a tune he was eager to compose, one honest note at a time.

## Reflection

After finishing this story, what are your own thoughts and feelings? Here are some questions to help you ponder the story's meaning and discuss its moral lessons with friends, family, or classmates.

### Question 1:
Jamie faced a tough decision when he found Mr. Harrison's whistle. Have you ever found something valuable that wasn't yours? What did you do, and how did it make you feel?

### Question 2:
When Jamie kept the whistle, he felt special and enjoyed the attention it brought him. Can you recall a time when you were tempted to keep something or a secret because it made you feel good, even though you knew it might not be right?

### Question 3:
Jamie felt guilty about taking the whistle. What are some signs that you might feel when you know you've done something wrong? How does your body tell you that you need to make things right?

### Question 4:
Do you think Jamie was brave to return the whistle? What does it mean to be brave, and how can admitting a mistake be an act of bravery?

### Question 5:
Mr. Harrison was understanding when Jamie returned the whistle and even shared a story of his own mistake. Why is it important to be forgiving when someone admits they were wrong?

### Question 6:
If you were Jamie's friend, what advice would you have given him when he first found the whistle? And what would you say after he returned it?

# The Test Day Mix-Up

## Ava's Discovery

Ava twirled her pencil, her eyes darting between the scribbles of study notes and the clock on the pale yellow wall of Pine Grove Elementary's classroom. The big test was just a day away, and the air buzzed with the collective nervousness of her classmates. It was the kind of test that could make or break your grade for the year, and nobody knew that better than Ava.

Straight As were Ava's trademark; they were as much a part of her as her curly brown hair and the smattering of freckles across her nose. And she worked hard for them. Ava wasn't just smart; she was diligent, poring over her books each night until the stars blinked sleepily outside her window.

Mrs. Henson, their teacher, paced the aisles between the desks, her heels clicking rhythmically on the tiled floor. "Remember," she said, her voice as smooth as the surface of the desk Ava was leaning on, "it's not just about memorizing facts. It's about understanding them, using them. That's what tests your true knowledge."

Ava nodded along with her classmates, but inside, her stomach was a tight knot. She understood alright, but the pressure was a high wall, and sometimes, understanding wasn't enough to scale it.

The bell rang, a shrill sound that signaled the end of the school day, and the students burst from their seats like birds from a cage. Ava, however, lingered. She had a question about one of the math problems, something she couldn't quite wrap her head around.

"Mrs. Henson?" Ava's voice was hesitant as she approached the teacher's desk.

"Of course, Ava. What's troubling you?" Mrs. Henson's eyes were kind, the sort that seemed to look right through to your problems.

As Ava laid out her question, pointing to the numbers that danced confusingly on the page, something else caught her eye. A slip of paper, peering out from a stack of books on Mrs. Henson's desk—it couldn't be. But the closer Ava looked, the clearer the printed words became. It was the answer key to tomorrow's test.

Ava's heart skipped a beat. She could easily slide it off the desk, slip it into her folder. No one would know. She could secure her As, no problem. It was the solution to all her worries, served up on a silver platter.

But even as the thought flickered through her mind, a wave of unease washed over her. She wasn't a cheater, was she?

"Is something wrong, Ava?" Mrs. Henson's voice pulled her back from the precipice of temptation.

Ava blinked, her gaze snapping up from the answer key to Mrs. Henson's face. "No, I... I think I just figured it out," she stammered, her voice barely a whisper.

"Are you sure?" Mrs. Henson peered at her with concern.

"Yes," Ava said, a little too quickly. "Thank you, Mrs. Henson. See you tomorrow."

She hurried out of the classroom, the image of the answer key seared into her memory. Tomorrow was the test, and Ava had a night to decide what to do. It was a decision that would test more than her knowledge—it would test her character.

## The Night of Choices

Ava's footsteps echoed down the empty hallway as she made her way out of Pine Grove Elementary. Her mind was a whirlwind, thoughts tumbling and colliding like leaves in a storm. The answer key felt like a heavy presence in her brain, and with every step, the weight of her discovery grew.

As she walked home, the world around her seemed to be in its own bubble of carefree routine. Cars hummed by, a dog barked in the distance, and the sun was dipping low, painting the sky in strokes of orange and pink. But Ava barely noticed. Her mind was stuck inside the classroom, hovering over the answer key that would make tomorrow's test a breeze.

Dinner was a quiet affair at Ava's house that night. Her parents chatted about their days, and her little brother, Max, excitedly shared his drawing of a dinosaur robot. Ava tried to engage, to laugh, to be part of the family moment, but her thoughts kept slipping away to the answer key, to the choice that lay before her.

Later, in the sanctuary of her room, Ava sat at her desk, her study notes scattered in front of her. She tried to focus, to prepare for the test as she always did, but the numbers and facts refused to stick. They were obscured by the bigger problem, the ethical math that wasn't so easily solved.

Ava lay in bed that night, the house quiet around her. The answer key was a shadow in the dark, its temptation a whispering voice that grew louder as the night deepened. She could almost hear it, calling to her, promising her an easy path, a path without hurdles or doubt.

But with every whispered promise came a stab of guilt. Ava thought of her classmates, of Mrs. Henson, of her family. She imagined their faces if they knew what she was considering. The disappointment in Mrs. Henson's eyes, the confusion in Max's, the hurt in her parents'—it was a mirror that reflected a version of herself she didn't recognize.

The night stretched on, and Ava turned restlessly, caught in the grip of her internal battle. The stars outside seemed to watch her through the window, their twinkle like questions that poked at her conscience. What kind of person did she want to be?

As dawn's first light crept across her bedroom floor, Ava's eyes opened. They were clear, decisive. She had made her choice. She knew what she had to do, not because it was easy, but because it was right. It was a decision that wouldn't just define her day but would define who she was going to be.

With determination in her steps, Ava readied herself for school. The answer key was no longer a temptation; it was a test she had passed before even stepping into the classroom. She had her integrity, her honesty, and that was the truest answer she needed.

## The Truth Unfolds

The morning air was cool as Ava made her way back to Pine Grove Elementary. The whispers of temptation that had haunted her through the night now lay silent, quelled by the resolve that marched firmly in her chest. She clutched her backpack straps tight, each step a beat in the rhythm of her decision.

The classroom was buzzing when Ava arrived, a hive of last-minute studying and frenzied recollections of facts and figures. Ava moved through the room like a ghost, her presence there but her mind elsewhere, focused on the task that lay ahead.

The bell rang, a signal that silenced the room, and Mrs. Henson entered with a stack of test papers under her arm. Her eyes swept across the class, landing on Ava with a soft smile. "Before we begin," she started, "does anyone have any last questions?"

Ava felt the moment had come. Her hand, as if of its own accord, rose into the air. A hush fell over the classroom, all eyes turning to her. "Mrs. Henson," Ava began, her voice a steady thread in the stillness, "there's something I need to say."

Mrs. Henson nodded, a gentle prompt for her to continue.

"I found the answer key to the test yesterday," Ava confessed, her heart thumping loudly in her ears. Murmurs rippled through the classroom like a wave, eyes wide, and heads turning.

Mrs. Henson's brow furrowed slightly, not in anger, but in intrigue. "Go on, Ava," she encouraged.

"It was an accident," Ava explained, "I saw it on your desk. But I didn't take it. I didn't use it. I wanted to tell you because it didn't feel right to keep it a secret." Her words hung in the air, brave and bold.

For a moment, the classroom was utterly silent, as if time itself had paused to acknowledge the gravity of her admission. Then, Mrs. Henson spoke, her voice clear and proud. "Ava, that took a lot of courage. Thank you for being honest with me, with all of us. This," she gestured to the class, "is what integrity looks like."

She turned to the rest of the class, her eyes sweeping over the sea of young faces now fixed on her. "Ava has given us a real-life example of what it means to be honest, to have character. The easiest path isn't always the right one. Sometimes, we face difficult choices, but it's what we do in those moments that define us."

Ava felt a flush of warmth spread through her as Mrs. Henson approached and gently took her hand, giving it a reassuring squeeze. The rest of the class was looking at her, no longer with curiosity, but with a newfound respect. Ava had exposed her vulnerability, her truth, and in doing so, she had elevated the importance of honesty for everyone around her.

"Now," Mrs. Henson announced, "let's start the test. Remember, you are all more than capable. Do your best, and know that it's your effort and honesty that truly count."

Ava took her test paper with hands that were now steady. As she looked down at the questions, she knew that she could answer them, not just with her mind, but with her heart, because today she had learned something far greater than what any test could measure. She had learned the value of her own integrity, and it was a lesson she would carry with her, long after the final bell rang.

## Reflection

After reading about Ava, it's time to reflect on the story and its deeper meaning. These questions are meant to help you think about the moral of the story and how it applies to your own life. You can think about these questions on your own, discuss them with your friends, or talk about them with your parents or teachers.

### Question 1:
Ava faced a tough decision when she found the answer key. Have you ever been in a situation where you had to choose between being honest or taking an easier but dishonest route? What did you choose and why?

### Question 2:
What does integrity mean to you? How do you think Ava's decision to tell the truth about the answer key showed integrity? Can you think of a time when you showed integrity?

### Question 3:
If Ava had used the answer key, what do you think might have happened? How would that choice have affected her, her classmates, and her teacher?

### Question 4:
Ava made her decision even though nobody else knew about the answer key. Sometimes, people around us can influence our decisions. Can peer pressure make it difficult to be honest? How can you deal with that pressure?

**Question 5:**
Ava did well on the test even without using the answer key. How do you think she felt about her score, knowing she earned it honestly? Have you ever felt proud of achieving something through hard work and honesty?

# The Farmer's Missing Apples
## The Orchard Adventure
Whispers of dawn crept over the sleepy farm as Chris and Riley met at their secret spot, the old wooden fence that bordered Mr. Jacobs' apple orchard. The sky painted a warm palette of oranges and pinks as the morning sun promised a day of endless possibilities.

"Race you to the big oak!" Riley challenged with a grin, his eyes sparkling with mischief.

"You're on!" Chris shouted back, and with a burst of energy, the two friends dashed across the dew-kissed fields, laughter trailing behind them like a kite on a string.

The farm was alive with the sounds of morning; roosters announcing the day, sheep bleating softly in the distance, and the gentle rustling of apple leaves in the soft breeze. Mr. Jacobs' orchard was a treasure trove of nature's sweets, rows upon rows of apple trees standing like sentinels guarding their ruby-red prizes.

As they reached the grand oak tree, Chris and Riley paused, their breaths coming out in short, excited puffs. They gazed at the apples with wide eyes, the fruit hanging temptingly from the branches, ripe and ready for picking.

"Wouldn't it be something to taste one?" Riley whispered, a cheeky smile spreading across his face.

Chris bit his lip, a battle of choices raging in his mind. He knew they shouldn't, but the apples looked so delicious, and adventure called to them like the wild hawks that circled above.

"Just one each," Chris agreed, the thrill of the forbidden making his heart race.

They looked around cautiously before slipping through a gap in the fence, the only witnesses to their caper being the sun and the silent trees. With the thrill of covert agents, they each plucked an apple, its skin smooth and cool in their guilty hands.

The fruit was everything the tales of summer promised—juicy, sweet, with a crunch that sang of secret orchard raids. But as the juice dripped down their chins, a shadow of doubt dimmed the glow of their triumph. They had taken something that wasn't theirs, and even the sun's golden rays couldn't chase away the chill of that thought.

As they left the orchard, the big oak tree stood tall behind them, its leaves whispering in the wind, a silent reminder of their morning's adventure. Little did Chris and Riley know that this day would start them on a journey—a journey that would teach them the value of honesty, and the price of a single apple.

## The Missing Apples

The afternoon sun cast long shadows across Mr. Jacobs' farm as he strolled through his beloved apple orchard, a woven basket swinging from his arm. He hummed an old tune, his eyes scanning the branches for the ripest of his apples. His fingers, weathered from years of tender care for his trees, reached out to cradle an apple, only to pause in mid-air. A frown creased his brow as he noticed a gap where a perfect apple should have been.

"Strange," he muttered to himself, his voice a low rumble like distant thunder.

As he continued his walk, his frown deepened. Here and there, apples were missing, not just fallen but vanished, as if plucked by invisible hands. His basket, usually brimming with the orchard's bounty, lay half-empty at his side. Mr. Jacobs' heart grew heavy, not from the loss of fruit, but from the trust he felt had been bruised.

The next morning, Mr. Jacobs took his old hat off and scratched his head, looking out over the faces of the local children gathered by the fence. They were a picture of innocence, with their curious eyes and fidgety hands, the farm's future he always said.

"Has anyone seen anything... unusual in the orchard?" he asked, his voice gentle yet tinged with an unspoken worry.

The children shook their heads, eyes wide, and Mr. Jacobs searched their faces for a clue, a sign, anything that could explain the mystery of his missing apples. But there was nothing, only the honest shrugs of shoulders and the silent language of children's puzzled glances.

In the back, barely noticeable, stood Chris and Riley, their eyes cast down, their hands knotted together. They felt the weight of Mr. Jacobs' gaze, heavy with the disappointment of unspoken words. The farmer's eyes lingered on them for a moment longer than the rest, a silent question hanging in the air.

The day wore on, and the children dispersed, leaving whispers and murmurs in their wake. Chris and Riley stayed behind, hidden in the shade of a large elm tree, their hearts pounding with the drumbeat of their secret.

"Maybe it's not that big of a deal," Chris said, trying to convince himself more than Riley.

But Riley's face was clouded with guilt. "We should tell him," he murmured, his voice barely above a whisper.

Chris shook his head, fear knotting his stomach. "We can't. What if he never trusts us again?"

The sun dipped lower in the sky, casting a golden glow over the farm. The boys watched Mr. Jacobs from their hiding spot, the farmer's shoulders stooped as he inspected his trees, the missing apples like silent accusations.

As night fell, the stars blinked to life above, indifferent witnesses to the turmoil churning in Chris and Riley's chests. The once-exciting secret now felt like a stone around their necks, and sleep was chased away by the shadow of their growing guilt.

## The Weight of Truth

The night passed with restless whispers, and dawn brought no relief to Chris and Riley. The farm was waking up, golden light spilling over the fields, but the joy of morning felt hollow. They met under the same old elm, their usual excitement replaced by a shared, sombre silence.

"We have to make it right," Riley declared, his decision firm like the ground under their feet.

Chris nodded, the burden of honesty growing heavier with the rising sun. "But how? We can't just say we took them."

Riley's eyes flickered with resolve. "We work for it. We show Mr. Jacobs we're sorry."

With the decision made, the boys approached Mr. Jacobs' porch, each step feeling like wading through a stream against the current. The farmer was there, his silhouette framed by the morning light, as he repaired a birdhouse, the soft tapping echoing the boys' anxious heartbeats.

"Mr. Jacobs?" Riley's voice quivered as they reached the bottom of the porch steps.

The tapping stopped. Mr. Jacobs looked up, his eyes soft but questioning. "Boys? What brings you here so early?"

Chris swallowed hard, his words tumbling out. "We have something to tell you. We took the apples, sir. And we're really sorry."

Silence fell, as dense as the fog that sometimes hugged the farm in the early hours. Mr. Jacobs set his tools down, his gaze never leaving the boys' faces.

"Why?" His question was simple, yet it held the weight of the world.

"We just... we didn't think," Riley stammered, "but we want to make it right."

Mr. Jacobs stepped down, his boots thudding softly on the wooden steps. He towered over them, a giant in both stature and heart. "You know, apples can be replaced, but trust, once broken, takes time to mend."

Chris and Riley hung their heads, the lesson piercing deeper than any scolding could.

"We want to work, to pay for what we took," Chris said, hope threading his voice.

The farmer's eyes held the boys for a long moment, searching, weighing, understanding. Then, slowly, he nodded. "Alright. Work starts tomorrow at dawn. We'll see about mending that trust."

Relief, swift and sweet, washed over Chris and Riley. They promised to work hard, to make up for their mistake, and with the farmer's forgiveness warming their backs, they walked home under a sky that promised second chances.

The farm settled into a quiet peace as night drew near, the apple trees standing tall and proud. But for Chris and Riley, the real work was just beginning, a journey not just of repairing trust but discovering the true value of honesty.

## Reflection

Take a moment to think about the story and what it means. These questions can help you reflect on the story's message and encourage discussions with your parents, teachers, or friends.

**Question 1:**
Why do you think Chris and Riley decided to take the apples from Mr. Jacobs' orchard? Reflect on what might have been going through their minds at that moment.

**Question 2:**
How did Chris and Riley feel after they took the apples? Think about how their feelings changed from when they first took the apples to when they decided to confess.

**Question 3:**
What made Chris and Riley decide to confess to Mr. Jacobs? What you think was the turning point for them.

**Question 4:**
How did Mr. Jacobs react when Chris and Riley confessed? Were you surprised by his reaction? Why or why not?

**Question 5:**
How do you think Chris and Riley's relationship with Mr. Jacobs changed after they confessed? Talk about trust and how it can be rebuilt.

# The Artist's Signature
## A Canvas of Possibilities

In the heart of a bustling classroom filled with the scent of paint and the hum of a dozen conversations, Eli dipped his brush into a pool of cobalt blue. With a steady hand and a serene expression, he swept the brush across his canvas, each stroke more confident than the last. The art room was his haven, a place where the whispers of doubt couldn't find him, where his imagination could dance across the canvas in leaps and twirls of vibrant color.

Around him, his classmates created their own worlds within the confines of stretched cotton and wooden frames. There was a buzz in the air, a symphony of creativity that was as intoxicating as the smell of fresh paint. Eli's painting—a tapestry of the setting sun dipping into a tranquil sea—drew quiet admiration from those who passed by. They paused, even if just for a moment, to lose themselves in the depths of the fiery oranges and soothing purples that Eli laid down with a natural ease.

Across the room, Sophie wrestled with her canvas, her brow furrowed, her lips a tight line. The blank space before her seemed to mock her, the daunting expanse of white a stark reminder of the ideas that refused to flow. She glanced over at Eli, her eyes tracing the easy way his hand moved, the way his painting came to life under his touch. A sigh escaped her lips, barely heard over the noise of the classroom.

As the afternoon shadows grew longer, casting geometric patterns across the art tables, the children began to pack away their brushes and palettes. Eli, lost in his art, didn't notice the time until the art teacher, Mrs. Maple, placed a gentle hand on his shoulder.

"Eli, it's beautiful," she said, her voice tinged with pride. She leaned closer, her eyes scanning the intricate details of his sunset. "Remember, a true artist always leaves a part of themselves on the canvas. Your signature, it's important."

Eli nodded, his cheeks flushed with the warmth of the praise. But before he could dip his brush into the black to sign his masterpiece, the shrill ring of the school bell pierced the air, and the moment was lost in the shuffle of students eager to escape.

"Tomorrow," he whispered to himself, placing his brush down. He would sign it then, when the paint was dry and the morning light lent its clarity to his work.

The classroom emptied, leaving behind the scent of turpentine and the ghostly echoes of laughter. Eli's painting, resplendent and bold, sat drying on an easel by the window, the bottom right corner untouched, waiting for the artist's final stroke, the signature that never came.

## The Unclaimed Masterpiece

The morning light spilled into the classroom through the tall, dust-flecked windows, washing over Eli's painting and setting the colors ablaze. The classroom was quiet in the early hour, the hustle of arriving students a muted murmur beyond the walls. Eli arrived early, his heart set on completing what he had started the day before. But as he approached his easel, he froze, his eager steps faltering.

Where his painting had been a canvas of his emotions, there now hung nothing but the ghost of its absence. His eyes darted around the room, searching, hoping for a glimpse of the familiar colors, but there was nothing. Panic clutched at his chest, his breath caught in his throat.

"Eli?" Mrs. Maple's voice cut through the thick haze of his worry. "Is something wrong?"

He turned to her, the words tumbling out in a rush. "My painting... it's gone."

Together, they searched, peering behind cabinets and opening closets, but it was clear. The painting had not been misplaced; it had been taken.

The bell rang, harsh and sudden, and the room filled with the clamor of students. Sophie slipped into the class amidst the chaos, her eyes downcast, her hands fidgeting with the straps of her backpack. She slid into her seat, and unlike the others, she didn't rush to set up her workspace. Instead, she sat still, her gaze lingering on a covered canvas that leaned against her desk, a secret hiding just beneath the white drape.

Eli's mind raced as he recounted the previous day, his eyes scanning the room, landing on each classmate, searching for a clue, any clue that might reveal where his painting had gone. Sophie's unusual quietness didn't go unnoticed, but his thoughts were interrupted before they could take shape.

"Class," Mrs. Maple announced, "we have a surprise. One of your classmates has brought in a painting they've been working on at home. Sophie, would you like to show us?"

There was a collective turning of heads, a symphony of chair legs scraping against the floor as the class's attention focused on Sophie. She hesitated, a visible tremor in her hands as she reached for the cloth.

With a flourish that didn't match her uncertainty, Sophie revealed the painting beneath. Gasps and murmurs filled the room. The colors, the strokes, the breathtaking sunset—it was Eli's painting, staring back at him with a boldness that felt like betrayal.

"That's... that's mine," Eli stammered, his voice a hollow echo of the shock that twisted inside him.

Sophie's eyes flicked to his, a flicker of something unreadable passing between them before she looked away. "No, it's not," she said, her voice a strange mix of defiance and something else, something like fear. "I painted it at home."

The class erupted into debates and questions. Some sided with Eli, others with Sophie, swayed by the signature that now claimed the bottom right corner: Sophie's name, written in a shaky hand.

Eli stood, his confusion giving way to a rising tide of hurt. He had always known that paintings could be copied, that art could be forged, but he had never imagined it would happen here, among friends, in the very place where he felt most at home.

The confrontation had been set into motion, an unstoppable force that would change the way Eli and Sophie saw themselves, and how the class would see them both.

## Colors of Confrontation

The clamor in the classroom had settled into a low hum, like bees around a hive, buzzing with the news of Sophie's claimed masterpiece. Eli's eyes were fixed on the painting, his heart sinking like a stone in a deep, dark lake. Around him, the walls of the art room seemed to close in, the chatter of his classmates an indistinct blur.

Mrs. Maple, sensing the tension, called for quiet. "Let's all take a step back," she suggested. Her eyes, kind but perceptive, met Eli's. "We'll sort this out," she assured, but the doubt that lingered behind her words was a shadow that fell coldly on Eli's heart.

The day trudged on, each minute stretching like wet canvas. Eli's thoughts were a tangle of brushstrokes, messy and overlapping. When the final bell rang, releasing them into the freedom of the corridor, Eli knew he couldn't leave things unresolved. He waited until the other students had filed out, their voices and footsteps fading down the hallway.

Sophie lingered, her fingers trailing over the painted canvas, her conflict written in the crease of her brow and the bite of her lip. Eli approached, his own nerves balled up in his fists.

"Sophie," he began, his voice firmer than he felt. "Why did you do it?"

Sophie jumped, her composure slipping. "Do what?" she asked, but her voice was too high, her stance too rigid.

"The painting," Eli said, his eyes never leaving the canvas that screamed his name in every brushstroke, despite the signature that betrayed him. "It's mine. You know it's mine."

Sophie's eyes darted to the door, to the windows, anywhere but Eli's accusing gaze. "I just... I found it," she stammered, her defense crumbling like dry clay. "It didn't have a name, and I thought..."

"That it wouldn't matter?" Eli finished for her, the hurt in his voice sharper than he intended.

A silence fell between them, heavy and uncomfortable. Sophie wrapped her arms around herself, as if holding in the truth was a physical effort.

"I thought maybe if I said it was mine," she whispered, finally, "then it would feel like it was."

Eli's anger wavered, the edge of it dulled by the raw honesty in her voice. He saw not just the lie, but the reason behind it. Sophie, with all her erased lines and half-finished sketches, had been searching for something too.

"I wanted to be seen," she said, her voice so soft it was almost lost in the shuffle of papers from the desk. "Like you are."

Eli's thoughts stilled. He saw not a thief, but a fellow artist lost among the shadows, yearning to step into the light. He remembered Mrs. Maple's words about leaving a part of oneself on the canvas. Had he, without meaning to, left a part of himself for Sophie to find?

The moment stretched on, the afternoon sun casting long shadows across the art room, the dust motes dancing in the beams like tiny stars.

"We need to tell Mrs. Maple," Eli said at last, his decision firm but not unkind.

Sophie nodded, a tear escaping down her cheek, leaving a streak as stark as a line of charcoal. "I know," she whispered. "I will. I'll tell everyone."

As they left the classroom together, the unsigned painting between them, Eli knew that the next day would bring a different kind of confrontation—one that would challenge not just Sophie's honesty, but the understanding of the entire class. But for now, they walked side by side, two artists, each signed by their actions, moving towards the uncertain promise of tomorrow.

## The Palette of Truth

The morning sun didn't just bring a new day to the art classroom; it cast a light on the courage it takes to face one's own mistakes. The usual clamor of chattering students was replaced by an unusual hush as Sophie stood in front of the class, her hands clasped tightly together, her painting—a beacon of both her wrongdoing and her resolve—resting on the easel beside her.

Mrs. Maple had given Sophie the floor, a gesture not just of discipline, but of learning and growth. The classroom was a cocoon, within which both failure and change were natural, inevitable. Eli watched from his seat, the storm of emotions from the day before settled into a quiet anticipation.

"I have something to say," Sophie's voice was a mere whisper, but in the stillness, it reached every corner. She took a deep breath, her next words stronger as she found her footing. "The painting," she glanced at Eli, seeking a silent forgiveness, "it's not mine. It's Eli's."

A ripple of whispers undulated through the classroom, but Sophie pressed on, her confession unwinding like the ribbons of color on a palette. "I found it, without a signature, and I..." she swallowed hard, "I wanted something to be proud of, so I lied."

Mrs. Maple's presence was a quiet anchor in the choppy waters of the classroom. "Why are you telling us this now?" she asked, her voice both stern and soft.

Sophie's eyes, which had been on the verge of tears, lifted, meeting those of her classmates. "Because it wasn't right. And because being honest is scarier than painting on a blank canvas, but it's also more important."

The class was silent, the truth of her words settling on them like the dust on their unused brushes. Eli felt a weight lift from his shoulders, a tension he hadn't fully recognized until it was gone. Sophie's admission was more than just the return of credit; it was an act of bravery he wasn't sure he could have mirrored.

Mrs. Maple moved to stand beside Sophie, her hand coming to rest on the young girl's shoulder. "It takes courage to admit when we are wrong," she addressed the class. "And it takes strength to forgive."

She turned to Eli. "And what do you say, Eli?"

All eyes were on him now, the silent pressure of expectation heavy in the air. Eli stood up, his own nervousness a fluttering bird in his chest. He walked to the front, standing opposite Sophie. The painting—the cause of so much turmoil—was just a backdrop now to something far more significant unfolding before them.

"I say," Eli paused, his eyes meeting Sophie's, "I say we learn from this. We all want to be seen, to be recognized for what we do. But it should be for the things we actually do, our own creations, not someone else's."

Sophie nodded, tears of relief rather than sorrow slipping down her face. "I'm sorry, Eli," she said earnestly.

Eli offered a small, genuine smile. "Let's make a new painting," he proposed. "One we can both be proud of, together."

The class erupted, not in whispers this time, but in applause. They understood. It wasn't just about the painting. It was about honesty, bravery, and the art of being true to oneself and others.

Mrs. Maple clapped her hands together, the sound crisp and clear. "Then it's settled. Let this be a lesson in honesty, in art, and in life. You both have shown great character today."

As Eli and Sophie turned to face the class, their shared smile was the true signature on the masterpiece of that moment—a lesson etched in the minds and hearts of all who witnessed it. The story of the unsigned painting would be one they'd tell for years, not because of the art that was created, but because of the honesty that was learned and the friendship that was painted in the truest colors of all.

## Reflection

Take a moment to reflect on the story and its messages. These questions can help you think more deeply about the themes of honesty, courage, and self-acceptance. They are also great conversation starters for discussions with parents, teachers, or classmates.

**Question 1:**
Why do you think Sophie decided to claim Eli's painting as her own? Have you ever been in a situation where being honest was challenging? How did you handle it?

**Question 2:**
Sophie eventually told the truth about the painting. How do you think she felt after confessing? Do you think it was easy for her? Why is it important to admit our mistakes?

**Question 1:**
How did Eli react when he found out Sophie took credit for his painting? What would you have done if you were in Eli's shoes? Why is understanding and forgiveness an important part of this story?

**Question 3:**
What did Sophie learn about herself by the end of the story? What did Eli

learn? Have you ever learned something important about yourself after a challenging situation?

**Question 4:**
Eli suggested making a new painting together with Sophie. Why do you think working together was a good idea? How can collaboration and teamwork help in resolving conflicts and building friendships?

**Question 5:**
If you were to discuss this story with a parent or teacher, what aspects of the story would you like to talk about? Are there any parts of the story that remind you of situations in your own life?

# The Whispered Rumor
## The Monster's Birth

Once upon a time, in a cozy neighborhood that buzzed with the sounds of endless summer, there stood a playground that was the heart of all childhood games. This was where friendships were forged over tag and hide-and-seek, where knees were scraped, and ice creams were shared under the watchful eyes of towering oaks and whispering pines.

Leo, with his mop of unruly hair and a smile that was always up to something, was the unspoken king of this little kingdom. His best friend Nina, with her braided hair and thoughtful eyes, was often by his side, a quiet but unmissable presence.

It was a day like any other, with the sun playing peek-a-boo through the leaves and the air filled with the sound of laughter, when Leo climbed atop the highest slide, his eyes twinkling with the day's mischief.

"Guess what I saw last night?" he called out, and all activity ceased, the air charged with anticipation. Leo was known for his stories, after all. He paused for effect, scanning the crowd of faces that turned to him with wide-eyed curiosity. "A monster," he declared, "in the woods right behind our playground!"

A collective gasp rose from the children as they huddled closer, their attention hooked. Leo's imagination danced wild and free as he described a creature with eyes like molten gold and a growl that could shake the leaves off the trees.

"It's fur was as black as night, and its claws," Leo continued, his voice lowering into a spine-tingling whisper, "as long as my arm!"

Nina, who was among the crowd, felt a frown crease her forehead. She knew Leo's tales were born from a kernel of fantasy, spun into a yarn for eager ears. But this felt different, and as she watched the faces around her turn from excitement to fear, she realized the power that stories could wield.

That night, as stars dotted the sky like splattered paint, the once lively sounds of the playground were absent. The swings stood still, and the slides were silent. A shadow of fear had descended upon the place that once buzzed with the pure joy of play.

In the quiet of his room, Leo felt the first stirrings of something he had not anticipated — a twinge of regret. He tossed and turned, trying to convince himself that it was just a story. Just a bit of fun.

But stories, he was soon to discover, had a way of growing teeth and claws when let loose into the world. And this monster was just beginning to stir.

## The Whispers Grow

The next morning, the playground awoke to an unusual hush. The early rays of sun found empty benches and untouched swings. A soccer ball lay abandoned mid-field, as if the game had vanished in a puff of smoke.

Leo arrived with the expectation of another day crowned as the king of adventures and the teller of tales. But instead of the usual chorus of cheers and challenges, he was met with wary looks and huddled whispers.

"Did you hear about the monster Leo saw?" one child murmured to another, not noticing Leo's approach.

"It must be huge! Have you seen how big Leo's arm is?" another replied, eyes wide with a mixture of fear and fascination.

Leo's chest puffed with pride at the ripples his story had caused. But as he looked around, he noticed the absence of laughter, the lack of scampering feet, and the empty slide that once served as his throne. A cold finger of doubt trailed down his spine.

Nina approached him then, her expression somber. "Leo, look at what your story has done," she said, gesturing towards the desolate playground. "This isn't exciting; it's scary."

"But it's just a story," Leo defended with a shrug, though the certainty in his voice was lost to the morning breeze.

"Stories can be powerful, Leo," Nina replied. "You have to fix this."

Leo wanted to argue, to laugh it off like he always did. But the image of the empty playground haunted him. He remembered the thrill of his friends' gasps, the wide-eyed wonder as they hung on his every word. It was supposed to be fun, wasn't it?

Throughout the day, Leo watched. He watched as children peeked nervously into the woods, as parents asked hushed questions, and as rumors grew into monstrous legends. The reality of his creation began to dawn on him. His story was no longer his — it had taken on a life of its own, a whispered rumor that held his friends in a grip of fear.

As the sun began to dip below the horizon, painting the sky with streaks of orange and pink, Leo sat alone on the cold metal of the slide. The echo of his own words rang in his ears. A monster. As black as night. Claws as long as my arm.

The thrill was gone, replaced by a hollow emptiness. Nina was right; he had to make things right. But how? How do you catch a rumor and stuff it back into the box? How do you kill a monster of your own making?

With the weight of his tale heavy on his shoulders, Leo realized the game had changed. It was no longer about being the center of attention. It was about being the hero he always pretended to be in his stories. And every hero, Leo knew, had to face their dragon. His dragon just happened to be a creature of his own whispers.

The night settled in, the stars hiding behind a veil of clouds, as if they too were afraid of the monster that lurked in the shadows of the children's imaginations. And in the quiet of the impending dark, Leo made a decision. It was time to face the beast.

## The Courage to Confess
As dawn's first light crept over the neighborhood, it found Leo already awake, sitting on the edge of his bed, his usual boundless energy replaced with a somber determination. Today was the day he would face the fears he had sown in the hearts of his friends.

He met Nina at the corner before they walked to school, her reassuring smile doing little to ease the knots in his stomach. "You can do this," she said. "Just tell them the truth."

The schoolyard was abuzz with the monster talk, the story growing more terrifying as each child added another layer to the legend. Leo felt the weight of every embellished detail, knowing it had all started with his own tall tale.

By lunchtime, Leo's resolve had solidified into a steely core. He could no longer sit back and watch the joy drain from his friends' faces, their playful spirits dimmed by an imaginary fear. With Nina at his side, he climbed atop the picnic table, his platform to set the record straight.

"Everyone, listen!" Leo's voice cut through the chatter, commanding the attention he once used to entertain. The schoolyard fell silent, eyes turning to the boy who had always had the best stories. But this time, Leo wasn't there to entertain; he was there to confess.

"There's something I need to tell you all," he began, the words heavy and unfamiliar. "The monster in the woods... it isn't real. I made it up." The admission hung in the air, stark and raw.

A wave of whispers rippled through the crowd. Shock, confusion, and then a dawning understanding passed over the faces of his classmates as they absorbed his confession.

"Why would you do that?" a voice called out, tinged with a mix of hurt and relief.

Leo took a deep breath, finding strength in Nina's encouraging nod. "I thought it would be fun, a story to tell. I didn't think it would go this far. I didn't think it would scare everyone." He looked down at his feet, then back up at the sea of faces. "I'm sorry. I'm really sorry."

It took a moment for his words to sink in. But then, something remarkable happened. Where fear and suspicion had once taken root, forgiveness began to bloom. One by one, his friends came forward, their expressions softening.

"We all get carried away sometimes," one said, a smile breaking through.

"Yeah, it's okay, Leo. We just want to play like before," another added, patting him on the back.

The bell rang, signaling the end of lunch, but the atmosphere had shifted. As the children filed back to class, the playground no longer felt like a place of shadows and fears. It had been restored to a place of joy and innocence, all because one boy had the courage to stand up and speak the truth.

As Leo and Nina walked side by side, a quiet understanding passed between them. Truth had triumphed, and with it, the real adventure had begun. The adventure of growing up, of being honest, and of facing the monsters we create—not with swords and shields, but with the hardest weapon of all to wield: the truth.

## Reflection

Take a moment to think about the story and what it means. These questions can help you reflect on the story's message and encourage discussions with your parents, teachers, or friends. Remember, there are no right or wrong answers, just thoughts and ideas to explore.

**Question 1:**
Why do you think Leo decided to make up the story about the monster in the first place? Reflect on what might have motivated Leo. Was it for fun, attention, or something else?

**Question 2:**
How did you feel when you learned that the children were scared to play outside because of Leo's story? Think about how rumors or stories can affect people's feelings and behaviors.

**Question 3:**
What do you think made Leo decide to tell the truth? Consider what might have influenced Leo's decision to confess. Was it his own feelings, Nina's advice, or seeing the consequences of his story?

**Question 4:**
If you were Nina, would you have done anything differently? Why or why not? Imagine yourself in Nina's position and think about how you would handle the situation.

**Question 5:**
Have you ever been in a situation where someone told a lie or a rumor? How did it make you feel? What did you do? Reflect on your own experiences with dishonesty and consider how it compares to the story.

**Question 6:**
Why is it important to tell the truth, even if the lie seems harmless at first? Discuss the impact of even small lies and why honesty is important.

Printed in Great Britain
by Amazon